LGBT
INTOLERANCE

BY A.W. BUCKEY

INTOLERANCE
AND VIOLENCE
IN SOCIETY

ReferencePoint
Press®

San Diego, CA

© 2020 ReferencePoint Press, Inc.
Printed in the United States

For more information, contact:
ReferencePoint Press, Inc.
PO Box 27779
San Diego, CA 92198
www.ReferencePointPress.com

LIBRARY OF CONGRESS CATALOGING-IN-PUBLICATION DATA

Name: Buckey, A.W., 1987– author.
Title: LGBT Intolerance/by A.W. Buckey.
Description: San Diego, CA: ReferencePoint Press, Inc., [2020] | Series: Intolerance and
Violence in Society | Audience: Grade 9 to 12 | Includes bibliographical references and index.
ISBN: 978-1-68282-685-0 (hardback)
ISBN: 978-1-68282-686-7 (ebook)
The complete Library of Congress record is available at www.loc.gov.

CONTENTS

IMPORTANT EVENTS IN THE HISTORY OF

INTOLERANCE AND VIOLENCE

1868
The word *homosexual* is first used to describe a person who primarily has same-sex desires.

1970
The first Pride March commemorates the anniversary of Stonewall. The march later becomes a global LGBT tradition.

1620s
European settlers bring anti-sodomy laws to the American colonies.

1948
The Kinsey Institute releases a report, *Sexual Behavior in the Human Male*, that suggests that many people have a mix of same-sex and opposite-sex desires.

1300s   1600s   1860   1940   1960

1952
Christine Jorgensen, a transgender woman, becomes the first American to undergo sex reassignment surgeries.

1300s
In Europe, anti-sodomy laws are used to punish people who engage in unlawful sex, including same-sex acts.

1969
A police raid on the Stonewall Inn, a gay bar in New York City, leads to six days of protests and activism by the New York LGBT community.

4

1987
Activists found ACT UP, an organization that uses acts of civil disobedience to raise awareness about the HIV/AIDS epidemic.

April 1974
Kathy Kozachenko becomes the first openly LGBT person elected to political office in the United States when she is elected to the city council in Ann Arbor, Michigan.

1997
Ellen DeGeneres becomes the first openly LGBT sitcom star when she and her TV character come out as being gay.

2015
Following the US Supreme Court's decision in *Obergefell v. Hodges*, same-sex marriage becomes legal in all fifty states.

1975　　1990　　2000　　2010　　2020

November 1974
Massachusetts state legislator Elaine Noble becomes the first openly LGBT person to be elected to a state office.

2003
The United States officially repeals all anti-sodomy laws that were used to target LGBT people.

2017
The murders of twenty-nine transgender people are recorded in the United States, the highest known number for any year.

1981
The first report is published about American victims of the HIV/AIDS epidemic, describing five cases of the deadly disease affecting young gay men.

2019
The Supreme Court upholds a policy banning transgender people from serving in the US military.

NOT SAFE
TO LEARN

In 2015, Liv Funk began her sophomore year at North Bend High School, a public school in the small coastal community of North Bend, Oregon. Like many high schoolers, she was dating a fellow student. Funk, who identifies as a lesbian, walked into the first day of school holding hands with her then-girlfriend. Almost immediately, they received stares and nasty comments from other people. Funk remembers that students and even teachers made negative comments to her and her girlfriend. Funk was bullied verbally and physically throughout high school for being a lesbian. Once, the school principal's son chased her and her girlfriend with his car, veering away at the last moment and yelling "faggot," an anti-gay slur, at the two of them.[1] At first, Funk tried to push past these incidents as part of high school life. But the bullying continued, and Funk's complaints to the principal were not addressed.

In Funk's junior year, she saw two boys yelling anti-gay slurs in an area just outside her school. When Funk asked them to stop, one of the boys said that he "hate[d] homos" and attacked Funk with his skateboard,

> "He said that he had homosexual friends, but because I was an open homosexual, I was going to hell."[3]
>
> —Liv Funk, remembering the words of a police officer at her school

Children who identify as LGBT or who are perceived by their peers as being LGBT are often bullied at school. School bullying is one of many forms of intolerance that LGBT people face.

injuring her hand.[2] Funk decided to report the attack to a police officer at her school. "The officer said that being gay was a choice, and it was against his religion," Funk recalls. "He said that he had homosexual friends, but because I was an open homosexual, I was going to hell."[3] Funk was stunned by this reaction. She felt unsafe with her fellow students and unprotected by the school's administration. At every level of the school, she faced hostility and discrimination because of her sexual orientation.

Funk's story is not unique. A 2017 study found that many LGBT teens regularly face bullying and discrimination. The acronym *LGBT* stands for "lesbian, gay, bisexual, and transgender." A *Q* which stands for "queer" or "questioning," is often included at the end of the acronym, making it *LGBTQ*. Lesbians are women and girls who primarily experience romantic and sexual attraction to people of the same sex. The word *gay* has historically been used for men who primarily feel same-sex attraction, although people of other genders use it too. Bisexual people experience attraction to both men and women, and transgender people identify with a gender different from the one they were assigned at birth. The word *queer* is often used as an umbrella term for people who identify as LGBT, and *questioning* refers to people who are figuring out their sexual and gender identity. People who primarily experience attraction to people of the opposite sex are known as *heterosexual* or *straight*, and people whose gender identities match the sex they were assigned at birth are known as *cisgender*. In 2017, the Human Rights Campaign, an organization that advocates for the LGBT community, conducted a survey of more than 12,000 US teens who identified as LGBTQ. The survey found that 70 percent of students had been bullied at school because of their sexual orientation. Only about one-quarter of students felt safe being open about their sexual orientation or gender identity at school. And only 5 percent of students felt that everyone on their school's staff supported LGBT students. Intolerant, unsafe school environments can have a devastating effect on students' health and well-being. Research shows that anti-LGBT bullying is associated with lower grades, a decreased likelihood of going to college, and higher rates of depression.

Despite the widespread epidemic of anti-LGBT bullying at US schools, there are no national laws that protect students from harassment based on sexual orientation or gender identity. Most states don't have laws specific to anti-LGBT bullying either. A 2016 study of LGBT discrimination in US schools noted that seven states had laws preventing students and teachers from discussing issues such as LGBT sexual health and discrimination in school, even though discussing these issues can be educational for students. At the time the report was published, only twenty states had laws against bullying students based on their sexual orientation or gender identity.

Oregon was one of those twenty states. Because of this legal protection, Funk and her ex-girlfriend Hailey Smith, who faced similar discrimination at North Bend High School, were able to file a complaint with the Oregon Department of Education. In 2018, a state investigation found that Funk and Smith, as well as other students, were the victims of discrimination based on their sexual orientation. As a result, the school's principal was fired. The police officer who told Funk she would go to hell was replaced. In addition, North Bend's school district had to create new policies aimed at protecting the rights and safety of LGBT students. Mathew dos Santos, a civil rights lawyer who was involved with the complaint, praised Funk's and Smith's bravery. "I don't think people always know how scary it can

> **"I don't think people always know how scary it can be to exist as LGBTQ+ in small towns."**[4]
>
> —Mathew dos Santos, civil rights lawyer

Despite facing intolerance, members of the LGBT community have found ways to publicly celebrate their identities together. Many LGBT Pride parades occur across the country each year.

be to exist as LGBTQ+ in small towns," he said. "What Liv and Hailey did was remarkable."[4] Funk graduated in 2018, but she is hopeful that the changes brought about by her complaint will help future students.

"When freshmen arrive in the fall, I want them to have a different experience: a school where everybody feels welcome and safe, no matter who they are or whose hand they happen to hold," she wrote in a blog post.[5]

There are many different forms of gender and sexual expression. Throughout history and in the present day, people with sexual orientations or gender identities that don't fit narrow norms have faced unfair treatment and even violence. The late twentieth century and the twenty-first century have seen many victories for the LGBT community. But discrimination against and exclusion of LGBT people, along with ignorance and hatred of LGBT experiences, still exist at every level of society. Today, activists, cultural leaders, and members of many communities are working to create a world in which LGBT people can live, study, work, and love freely.

WHAT IS THE HISTORY BEHIND

LGBT INTOLERANCE?

Novelist E. M. Forster was born in England in 1879. From a young age, Forster knew he was attracted to other men. He kept his desires secret and wrote novels about relationships between men and women. Forster had his first sexual experience in his late thirties and later fell in love with a male train conductor. After he accepted the truth of his sexuality, Forster wrote less for the public. His only novel discussing love between men was published after his death, although it had been written fifty years earlier. Forster's long, secretive path to love and happiness led him to reflect on the lives of others who kept their sexuality secret. "I see beyond my own happiness and intimacy," Forster wrote, "occasional glimpses of the happiness of 1000s of others whose names I shall never hear, and I know that there is a great unrecorded history."[6]

Forster's words point to a difficult truth about LGBT history. Members of the LGBT community have often had to keep their identities and relationships secret in order to survive. This means countless details of LGBT history will always be unknown. In addition, norms of sexual orientation (the gender or genders a person is attracted to), gender identity (the gender a person identifies as), and gender expression (the ways in which a person lives out gender identity) vary greatly throughout history. There have always been people who loved others of the same sex and people who identified outside of traditional gender norms. At the same time, members of the LGBT community have faced powerful cultural, institutional, and personal barriers to safety and inclusion.

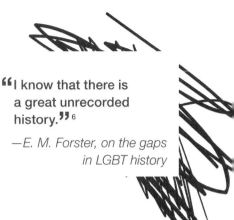

"I know that there is a great unrecorded history." 6

—E. M. Forster, on the gaps in LGBT history

EARLY IDEAS OF GENDER AND SEXUALITY

Gender fluidity, or the idea that there are gender identities that shift between or exist beyond male and female, is not a new concept. Many ancient civilizations worshipped gods who could change gender or combine characteristics from more than one sex. The ancient Norse god Loki could change from male to female, bearing children in the female form. The Middle Eastern goddess Ishtar had a similar power, but she could also change the gender of others. Many Hindu gods and goddesses also displayed gender fluidity.

In ancient Greece and Rome, it was common and accepted for mature men to take younger men as their lovers. There are also artistic and historical records of sexual love between women, although these relationships were not considered as acceptable by society. Many other ancient cultures accepted same-sex relationships, as long as the people in these relationships also fulfilled the roles of heterosexual marriage and childrearing. For example, in China around 20 BCE, an emperor named Ai was well known for his lack of interest in women and love for a married male member of the court. One legend describes Ai and his lover, Dong Xian, napping together. The emperor got ready to get up but couldn't bear the thought of waking Dong Xian, who was resting on his sleeve. Instead, the emperor cut the sleeve of his own robe off. "The passion of the cut sleeve" became a coded reference to sexual and romantic love between men.[7]

PRE-MODERN GENDER AND SEXUAL NORMS

In pre-modern Europe, most people followed strict sexual and gender norms influenced by Christianity and traditional cultures. Men and women followed separate rules for gender expression. Men dressed in gender-specific clothing, and women were expected to look traditionally feminine. Men and women had different jobs and household roles. However, there are records of people who lived outside of these rules. Saint Marinos, or Marina the Monk, was born female but lived as a male monk in fifth-century Lebanon. Historians have found evidence that some early Christian churches may have blessed same-sex unions between men. However, most European Christian societies followed sexual norms that did not allow same-sex love and intimacy. Sex was only accepted as an act between husbands and wives for the purpose of producing children.

These sexual standards were often enforced with anti-sodomy laws. The word *sodomy* comes from the Biblical city of Sodom. The Christian Bible's Book of Genesis describes the people of Sodom as "sinning greatly," but it does not describe what their sins were.[8] Over time, many came to understand the crimes of Sodom as unlawful sexual acts, generally oral or anal sex. In the Middle Ages, sodomy became a crime that could be punished by death in some circumstances. While anti-sodomy laws were often applied to heterosexual acts, they began to be used to forbid sex between men in the 1600s. The European colonists who overtook North America brought European Christian sexual and gender norms with them. In 1636, an influential Massachusetts preacher suggested that sex between women should be considered sodomy as well. In the colonial United States, there were at least two cases of women being punished for having sex with other women. Hundreds of years later, in the 1960s and 1970s, many US states continued to use anti-sodomy laws to penalize LGBT people, particularly gay men. These laws were used to prevent gay people from raising children or visiting their own children, to oppress them in the workplace, and to prevent them from speaking out against discrimination. For example, until the

We'Wha became a well-known representative of the Zuni people and met President Grover Cleveland in 1866. We'Wha was born male but embraced traditionally feminine characteristics.

twenty-first century, Virginia and Mississippi courts used anti-sodomy laws to deny gay parents custody of their own children, portraying the parents as criminals. In 2003, a US Supreme Court ruling declared these anti-sodomy laws unconstitutional.

Along with recorded accounts of same-sex relationships, there are also accounts throughout US history of people dressing and living as a gender other than the one they were assigned at birth. In the 1890s, a man named Frank Blunt was convicted of theft in Wisconsin. After his arrest, Blunt was revealed to have been born female.

In several Native American cultures throughout history, there have people who lived in gender roles that were neither traditionally male nor female. Today, people in many Native American cultures call this *two spirit*. We'Wha, a potter from the Zuni people in New Mexico, was born male but embraced many traditionally feminine roles. In 1866, We'Wha traveled to Washington, DC, and met President Grover Cleveland, who perceived We'Wha as female.

SEXUALITY RESEARCH

While there have always been people who love others of the same sex, the words *homosexual* and *heterosexual* are relatively recent. Historians believe the word *homosexual* was first used in 1868. The late 1800s and early 1900s marked a change in many Western societies' understandings of sexuality. Rather than viewing same-sex intimacy as simply a behavior, people began to see homosexuality and heterosexuality as personal identities. Still, the identities that LGBT people were expected to conform to at that time were often narrow, limiting, and considered by society to be sick or disordered. For example, one common concept of LGBT identity from this time was the invert. Inverts were understood to be people who had the soul of one sex, trapped inside the body of another. A male invert, for example, had a woman's personality, gender expression, and sexual desire (for men), but the body of a man. This concept of sexual and gender identity failed to capture the differences between gender expression, gender identity, and sexual orientation that are more commonly recognized today.

Gender expression, gender identity, and sexual orientation are different facets of a person's identity. However, they are often discussed together. This is partly because many traditional ideas of male and female identity include expectations for sexual desire and behavior. In other words, in many cultures, men are traditionally expected to see the desire and pursuit of women as part of their gender identity and expression, and women are expected to see sexual desire for men as part of their gender identity and expression. These expectations are called *heteronormativity*, a word that refers to the normalization of heterosexual identity. Men and women who desire and pursue same-sex intimacy have often been seen as breaking these norms, even if they fit traditional norms of gender identity and expression in other ways. In a similar way, people who express their gender in nontraditional ways are often assumed to have same-sex desires, even if this is not the case.

Alfred Kinsey, an American sexuality researcher and scientist, was interested in the ways that people's private sexual behavior might differ from the gender and sexual norms they accepted in public. In 1947, Kinsey founded the Institute for Sex Research. The following year, Kinsey released a report called *Sexual Behavior in the Human Male*. Based on interviews and research, Kinsey and his colleagues had found that about 10 percent of American men had only had sexual experiences with other men in the past three years. More than one-third of men had had some kind of sexual contact with a person of the same sex. Kinsey's later research on women found that about 2 to 6 percent of young women were only sexually active with other women, while 13 percent had had same-sex experiences. Kinsey's methods have been criticized and questioned by other researchers, largely because his study was only of white men, and he did not select his interviewees at random. Nevertheless, his proposal that many people were neither exclusively gay nor exclusively straight was influential. Kinsey developed a Heterosexual-Homosexual Rating Scale, now known as the Kinsey Scale. Instead of sorting people into the two categories of homosexual or heterosexual, the scale

placed all people somewhere on a spectrum of sexual orientation. "The living world is a continuum in each and every one of its aspects," Kinsey wrote. "The sooner we learn this concerning human sexual behaviour, the sooner we shall reach a sound understanding of the realities of sex."[9] Kinsey's research focused on cisgender people.

> **"The living world is a continuum in each and every one of its aspects. The sooner we learn this concerning human sexual behaviour, the sooner we shall reach a sound understanding of the realities of sex."** [9]
>
> —*Alfred Kinsey, sexuality researcher*

THE EARLY TRANSGENDER MOVEMENT

People can use names, clothing, activities, and mannerisms to express a gender identity other than the sex they were assigned at birth. In addition, some people take on different gender identities in different times and places. For example, one common tradition in many cultures is the use of crossdressing, or wearing the traditional clothes of the opposite sex in theatrical performances or rituals. Other people have a gender identity that differs from their sex assigned at birth. Today, the adjective used to describe these people is *transgender*. The word *transgender* is even newer than *heterosexuality* and *homosexuality*. The first known uses of *transgender* date back to the 1960s. Before *transgender* became an accepted term, people whose sex or gender identity differed from what was assigned at birth were called *transsexuals*.

Around the turn of the twentieth century, doctors began to explore medical therapies that would allow people more freedom to present themselves physically as a gender they were not assigned at birth. German doctor Magnus Hirschfeld began advocating for

THE HOUSE OF LABEIJA

Around 1960, a new tradition emerged in the LGBT scene in Harlem, New York City. Gay and trans people, most of whom were black and Latinx, began performing at balls. Performers at balls wear outfits that display a variety of gender expressions. The practice of taking on the gender expression of another sex through clothes and make-up is sometimes called *drag*. Harlem balls include drag performances and dancing. Young members of the ball scene often join houses. Houses are groups that mentor and connect young LGBT people in the community. They are led by a mother, an elder in the ball scene who does not necessarily identify as a woman.

The oldest of these houses is the House of LaBeija, founded in 1977 by drag performer Crystal LaBeija. Members of the house take the last name LaBeija as their own. At first, these houses were in-person social networks based in New York City. Today, they have spread geographically, and as of early 2019, the House of LaBeija had more than 100 members across the world. One member, Thunder LaBeija, sees the house as a source of comfort and safety. "Us having a bond outside of the ballroom scene is where we learn more about each other," Thunder says. "I have a big, beautiful, and dysfunctional family."

Quoted in Andrew Nguyen, "50 Years of Chosen Family," The Cut, January 25, 2019. www.thecut.com.

medical procedures to help transgender people live more fully in their identities. The first person to undergo surgery to present herself more easily as a woman was a Danish painter named Lili Elbe. Elbe, born in 1882, lived as a man until adulthood, when she began dressing in women's clothes and discovering her female gender identity. From 1930 to 1931, Elbe underwent new surgeries to remove her penis and testicles and replace them with ovaries and a uterus. She died in 1931 after complications from one of the surgeries.

In 1952, Christine Jorgensen became the first American woman to undergo a medical change of gender. She took hormones and had surgeries to give her body a more traditionally female appearance. Jorgensen became a celebrity, giving speeches and writing a memoir. The same year, a group of American trans women began the first published journal for transgender people and crossdressers, *Transvestia*. In the 1960s and 1970s, transgender people began organizing political action groups. However, transgender activists were frustrated to find their concerns often sidelined within the larger LGBT rights movement. During this time, some feminists came out as anti-transgender, falsely portraying transgender men as traitors and transgender women as men in disguise threatening women's communities. Because of the stigma against transgender people, some lesbian, gay, and bisexual activists believed they would be more successful with the larger public if they focused only on the concerns of gay cisgender Americans.

THE STONEWALL UPRISING

Until the later half of the twentieth century, US medical professionals generally agreed that being gay was a mental illness. Some gay and lesbian people went through what was then considered medical treatment for their sexuality. These treatments used painful methods such as electric shocks, sterilization, and in some cases lobotomies, or partial removals of the brain. Homosexuality was officially removed from the *Diagnostic and Statistical Manual of Mental Disorders*, the national standard medical book of mental disorders, in 1973.

By 1969, every state except Illinois had a law against gay sex. It was dangerous for most LGBT people to be honest about their sexuality in public. But at the same time, LGBT people were creating communities and traditions of their own. Many LGBT communities centered around certain bars and nightlife spots in major cities. These were places where LGBT people could go after work or school to meet other members of the LGBT community and gather in a relatively safe space. Police officers would often raid LGBT bars, arresting some of the people there and intimidating others. The police had the power to publish the names of people they found at LGBT bars.

One of these raids happened at the Stonewall Inn in Greenwich Village, New York City, on June 28, 1969. In the middle of the night, New York City police began to arrest bar patrons. Then, something surprising happened. The people at the bar started fighting back. "That night, the police ran from us . . . and it was fantastic," one person remembered in an interview.[10]

That night sparked a series of protests by LGBT communities known as the Stonewall Uprising. The protests lasted for more than six days. Activists Marsha P. Johnson and Sylvia Rivera were at the forefront of the Stonewall Uprising and helped advocate for the inclusion of trans rights in the larger gay rights movement. Johnson and Rivera, who were both sex workers and performers in New York, advocated for trans people, LGBT people of color, and homeless LGBT youth. While they did not always identify as transgender, they had female gender expressions and aligned with the transgender movement.

The Stonewall Uprising helped begin a new era for LGBT visibility and advocacy. Groups such as Daughters of Bilitis, a lesbian organization, and Lambda Legal, a nonprofit legal organization,

Years after the Stonewall Uprising, the Stonewall Inn is still open in New York City. It remains an important, historical symbol for the LGBT community, and it officially became a national monument in 2016.

started to push for greater rights for LGBT people. The first continually operating LGBT newspaper, the *Advocate*, was also founded around this time.

The 1970s saw the election of the first openly LGBT public servants. In 1974, Kathy Kozachenko won a city council seat in Ann Arbor, Michigan, becoming the first openly LGBT American in an elected position. But while this era saw a lot of progress, there was also backlash. Harvey Milk became a national figure in 1978 when he was elected as a city supervisor in San Francisco, California, becoming the first openly gay man to be elected to political office in the United States. But he was murdered later that same year.

Also during the 1970s, conservative and religious groups campaigned against the acceptance of LGBT people. Some public

> "What [LGBT people] really want . . . is the legal right to propose to our children that theirs is an acceptable alternate way of life. I will lead such a crusade to stop it as this country has not seen before."[11]
>
> *—Anita Bryant, 1970s anti-gay activist*

figures, such as singer Anita Bryant, helped popularize the idea that LGBT people were dangerous to children. "What [LGBT people] really want . . . is the legal right to propose to our children that theirs is an acceptable alternate way of life," Bryant said. "I will lead such a crusade to stop it as this country has not seen before."[11]

ACT UP AND THE AIDS CRISIS

In the early 1980s, doctors became aware of five young and previously healthy men who had either died from or become severely ill with a rare infection. These men, who were all gay, had weakened immune systems. In 1982, the immune-system destroying condition was first identified as acquired immunodeficiency syndrome (AIDS). By 1987, 40,000 people in the United States were infected with human immunodeficiency virus (HIV), the infection that can develop into AIDS.

HIV is transmitted through contact with bodily fluids such as blood and semen. Members of the LGBT community were disproportionately affected by the disease. Men who had unprotected sex with other men were at a high risk of contracting the disease. Unprotected sex between men had wrongly been perceived as low risk because there is no risk of pregnancy. Because gay and bisexual communities were relatively small, the disease spread quickly among men sexually active with other men. By 1987, people understood how HIV spread, and it was common knowledge that HIV cannot be contracted by simply touching or being around another person. Still, there was widespread stigma against people with AIDS and misinformation about the disease. Homophobia and transphobia, or the hatred of LGBT people, intensified this stigma. Many people lacked compassion for people who had contracted the disease through same-sex sexual activity. Some people refused to touch or associate with people infected by AIDS. Businesses and schools discriminated against people with AIDS, and AIDS patients faced barriers to effective health care.

By 1982, the organization Gay Men's Health Crisis had formed in New York City to help respond to the epidemic. They were furious and heartbroken by what they saw as public indifference to a deadly epidemic. The organization ACT UP, founded in 1987, worked to raise awareness about the AIDS epidemic by any means necessary. Their slogan was "Silence = Death," and their symbol was a pink triangle.[12] ACT UP committed acts of civil disobedience such as delivering coffins to public officials. The organization successfully boycotted companies that refused to serve customers with AIDS. Historians credit ACT UP and other activist organizations for bringing the AIDS crisis to public attention and helping to push for research and treatment of the disease. The movement also helped show the power and commitment of the LGBT community in the face of an overwhelming threat. By October 1995, there had been 500,000 reported cases of AIDS in the United States.

THE SAME-SEX MARRIAGE MOVEMENT AND OTHER LEGAL BATTLES

In the 1980s and 1990s, it became more common for LGBT people to openly acknowledge their identities. A new tradition emerged: "coming out of the closet."[13] The phrase, often abbreviated to *coming out*, means publicly acknowledging one's own LGBT identity. Throughout the 1990s, it became increasingly common for celebrities and public figures to come out and for LGBT people to be able to comfortably live their lives without concealing their identities.

Nevertheless, intolerance against the LGBT community remained common. The electroshock and other painful therapies of the mid-twentieth century were no longer considered legitimate medical treatments. However, they endured in the form of conversion therapy, or physical and psychological treatments meant to prevent people from being LGBT.

Violence against the LGBT community also continued. In 1998, a young gay man named Matthew Shepard was murdered in Laramie, Wyoming, by two young men. In 2009, Shepard's death, along with the murder of James Byrd Jr., a black man killed in a racist attack, were the inspirations for the Matthew Shepard and James Byrd Jr. Hate Crimes Prevention Act, a law that gives law enforcement greater funding to investigate crimes motivated by prejudice and hate.

In the 2000s and 2010s, one of the largest frontiers for LGBT rights was the fight for marriage equality. Legalization of same-sex unions began on the state level, with civil unions and same-sex marriages gaining recognition in several states. A civil union is a partnership between people that is similar to a legal marriage. Traditionally, legal marriages offer benefits such as the ability to inherit a spouse's property or save on certain taxes. Like marriages, civil unions offer couples some similar protections. Unlike marriages, civil unions are only recognized by one state, not by the entire country. Before same-sex marriage was legal nationwide, some states offered civil unions as an alternative. In the 2015 decision *Obergefell v. Hodges*, the Supreme Court ruled 5–4 that same-sex marriage should

Same-sex marriage became legal in the United States in 2015. That change was widely viewed as a major victory for the LGBT community.

be legal in all fifty states. "Changed understandings of marriage," the opinion read, "are characteristic of a Nation where new dimensions of freedom become apparent to new generations."[14]

By 2017, 70 percent of Americans said they would support laws to address intolerance against the LGBT community. Many people saw the *Obergefell v. Hodges* decision as a decisive victory for LGBT rights. But some point out that LGBT intolerance is still deeply entrenched in US society. As of 2018, almost half of all Americans believed wedding businesses should be able to refuse service to same-sex couples. Support for same-sex marriage has greatly increased since 2015, but as of 2017, 28 percent of Americans opposed same-sex marriage. In 2018, a Gallup poll found that 30 percent of responders believed same-sex intimacy was morally wrong.

HOW IS SOCIETY INTOLERANT OF
LGBT PEOPLE?

According to a 2017 Gallup poll, 4.5 percent of Americans identify as LGBT. Young people are more likely to describe themselves as LGBT. The poll found that 8.1 percent of millennials, people born between 1980 and 1999, identify as LGBT. Five percent of all women and 4 percent of all men responded that they were LGBT. Research from the Williams Institute found that African American and Latinx people are more likely to identify as LGBT than white people are. A 2011 survey by the Williams Institute estimated that approximately 0.3 percent of Americans identified as transgender. According to the Williams Institute, LGBT people are most likely to live in the West, the Northeast, and the Southeast regions of the United States. Gallup found that the greater San Francisco area has the highest percentage of its population identifying as LGBT, at 6.2 percent. Birmingham, Alabama, is the city with the lowest concentration of LGBT people, at 2.6 percent. As a whole, compared with Americans who do not identify as LGBT, members of the LGBT community make slightly more money, are equally as likely to have a college degree, and are less likely to be raising children.

There is vast diversity among members of the LGBT community, but they still face many common challenges. LGBT people

LGBT people of color often face more discrimination than white members of the LGBT community. Discrimination can happen at home, at work, and in public places.

confront intolerance in many forms, from personal bias to systemic discrimination. Intolerance against LGBT people occurs in unfair treatment and biased attitudes that people must endure as part of daily life. In some cases, this intolerance takes the form of exclusion, such as from events, relationships, and jobs. LGBT people face discrimination in families, workplaces, religious spaces, the media, and elsewhere.

LGBT DISCRIMINATION IN FAMILIES

When Mark Shrayber was a child, his parents used to take their out-of-town visitors to the Castro, a famous LGBT neighborhood in San Francisco. The family would stare at the gay people there and say they were strange. Shrayber knew his parents believed that being gay was worse than having cancer or being addicted to drugs. In high school, Shrayber was homophobic, like his parents, and he bullied a gay student. But eventually he could not hide the truth about himself. His father once told him, "One day, Mark, you will say, 'Daddy, I am gay,' and you will not be a part of this family anymore."[15] Shrayber came out as gay to his parents at the age of eighteen. They eventually made peace with his sexuality, though they sometimes still asked if their son would be gay "forever."[16]

Shrayber is not alone in his experiences. LGBT people often have their first experience of intolerance in their own families. Families may decide to shun or kick out an LGBT family member. They may accept only parts of the family member's life, refusing to meet their LGBT loved one's partners or discuss their sexuality. Many children come to learn that they are loved and accepted in their families only when they can hide or minimize their true identities.

Writer Sarah Schulman, who is a lesbian, discusses the homophobia that young LGBT people experience in families in her book *Ties that Bind*. When Schulman's father found her with a female lover in her teens, she remembers, "He humiliated me in front of my brother and sister and put the shunning process into effect."[17] Although Schulman tried many times to establish a close and open relationship with her parents, they were unable to accept her identity and relationships.

Other parents restrict LGBT adults' access to children or seek to keep LGBT people from becoming parents. They may claim that a person who identifies as LGBT is inherently unhealthy for children. Several decades after Anita Bryant's famous anti-LGBT activism, some people still believe that LGBT people should not be allowed to parent or mentor children. Schulman's sister has inherited their

67%

67% of LGBT youth hear their families make negative comments about LGBT people

78%

78% of LGBT youth who have not come out to their parents hear their families make negative comments about LGBT people

48%

48% of LGBT youth who have come out to their parents say their families make them feel bad for identifying as LGBT

24%

24% of LGBT youth feel they can openly express their LGBT identity at home

25%

25% of LGBT youth have families who show support for them by getting involved in the larger LGBT and ally community

Family relationships can affect teenagers' self-esteem and mental health. According to the Human Rights Campaign, many LGBT teenagers report being extremely stressed out by the idea of coming out to their families. Much of this stress comes from hearing their family members make negative comments about LGBT people. LGBT youth of color report hearing these negative comments more often than their white peers. Once they are out to their families, the stress for LGBT youth often continues. Trans youth are particularly affected, as they are two times more likely to be taunted or mocked by their families than cisgender lesbian, gay, or bisexual youth. Only about one-quarter of LGBT youth report receiving strong family support for their sexual orientation or gender identity.

"2018 LGBTQ Youth Report," Human Rights Campaign, *2018. www.hrc.org.*

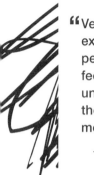

> **"Very few [gay people] experience their personhood, lives, and feelings to be actively understood as equal to the heterosexual family members."** [18]
>
> —Sarah Schulman, writer and activist

parents' homophobic attitude and does not allow Schulman to be alone with her children.

Schulman also notes that discrimination can come in more subtle forms, such as being treated with second-class status at family events. "Very few [gay people]," Schulman writes, "experience their personhood, lives, and feelings to be actively understood as equal to the heterosexual family members."[18] She believes even when people do not openly discriminate against LGBT family members, they should still be held accountable for tolerating the unequal treatment of their loved ones who identify as LGBT.

LGBT DISCRIMINATION IN THE WORKPLACE

According to US law, it is illegal for employees to sexually harass each other at work. This definition of *sexual harassment* includes harassing someone because of their gender identity, gender expression, or sexual orientation. However, there is no national law that protects employees from discrimination on the basis of sexual orientation, gender identity, or gender expression. This means that, in most states, employees can be fired simply for identifying as LGBT. A 2015 survey by the National Center for Transgender Equality found that transgender people were three times more likely to be unemployed compared with cisgender people. A 2008 study found that one-quarter of LGBT people had experienced employment discrimination in the past five years.

In 2017, art teacher Stacy Bailey introduced herself to her fourth-grade classroom. As part of a short presentation about her life, she showed a picture of her partner, Julie Vasquez, and explained that they were getting married. Shortly afterward, Bailey was suspended from her job and was told that she had shown "inappropriate images to children."[19] The school claimed that by showing a picture of her fiancée, Bailey had inappropriately pushed her personal beliefs onto the students. One parent complained, "I am afraid the girls love the teacher so much that someday they will want to do that," referring to Bailey's relationship with another woman.[20] Bailey filed a lawsuit alleging discrimination on the basis of her sexual orientation. In the fall of 2018, Bailey was given a new position at the school district, this time with high school students. Bailey and her lawyer believe that the new position, in a larger classroom with older students, is intended to frustrate her and convince her to quit her job. According to a 2011 report by GLSEN, an LGBT education advocacy organization, most teachers who identified as LGBTQ believed that being open about their identities with students would put their jobs at risk. One-quarter of these teachers had experienced harassment at work.

In some cases, discrimination can drive talented workers away from their jobs. Meagan Hunter was a server at a Chili's restaurant in Arizona. She was great at her job and interested in advancing within the company, which led to the opportunity to attend a seminar for Chili's employees who were interested in management jobs. At the seminar, Hunter wore clothes that fit her gender expression—a men's button-down shirt and slacks. Hunter prefers to dress in men's formal clothing and does not feel comfortable in traditionally feminine clothes. Although her outfit was similar to the clothes that men wore at the seminar, Hunter was told later that her outfit was "inappropriate."[21]

PROPOSITION 8

In 2008, the same-sex marriage movement was still underway in the United States. Only Massachusetts, Connecticut, and New Jersey had legalized same-sex unions. However, the state of California had a long history of activism in favor of same-sex unions. In 1984, the California city of Berkeley was the first place in the United States to pass a domestic partnership law that gave some legal protections to same-sex couples. In 2008, the California Supreme Court ruled that same-sex marriage should not be banned in the state. This meant that Americans who married a partner of the same sex in another state or country would have their unions recognized in California. However, the court's 2008 ruling sparked a backlash in California. In response, activists began campaigning for a California constitutional amendment that would ban same-sex marriage. Proposition 8 was a ballot measure that would allow California residents to vote on this proposal. More than $83 million was spent on public campaigning either for or against this proposition. In the end, Proposition 8 passed, and same-sex couples in California could not have their marriages recognized until the measure was overturned in 2010. In 2015, same-sex marriage became legal in all fifty states by a US Supreme Court ruling. The story of Proposition 8 helps show that progress in favor of LGBT rights has often been uneven, and that progress comes with backlash and struggle.

Later, Hunter found that she had been passed over for a bartender position at the same restaurant because the manager "didn't want a gay girl behind the bar."[22] Hunter ended up quitting her job because she did not see a way forward for her career.

Some LGBT employees may decide to keep their identities secret at work rather than face open discrimination and bias. But keeping this secret takes its own toll. Louise Young is a software engineer and LGBT activist. Early in her career, she lost her job after the company discovered she'd visited a lesbian bar socially, outside of work.

She went on to create a Lesbian, Gay, Bisexual, Transgender and Allies employee group at another employer, Raytheon. Young urges her colleagues to consider the effects of LGBT exclusion in the workplace. "You cannot talk about your family and where you went on vacation," she says. "If your spouse or partner is seriously ill, you are afraid to acknowledge your relationships because you're afraid you might lose your job. Do all that and see how productive you are."[23]

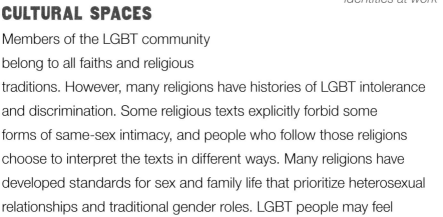

"If your spouse or partner is seriously ill, you are afraid to acknowledge your relationships because you're afraid you might lose your job. Do all that and see how productive you are."[23]

—*Louise Young, protesting expectations that LGBT people not discuss their sexualities and gender identities at work*

LGBT INTOLERANCE IN RELIGIOUS AND CULTURAL SPACES

Members of the LGBT community belong to all faiths and religious traditions. However, many religions have histories of LGBT intolerance and discrimination. Some religious texts explicitly forbid some forms of same-sex intimacy, and people who follow those religions choose to interpret the texts in different ways. Many religions have developed standards for sex and family life that prioritize heterosexual relationships and traditional gender roles. LGBT people may feel as if they must make painful choices between staying faithful to their religion and pursuing the romantic and sexual relationships they desire.

Savannah is a teenage girl who belongs to the Church of Jesus Christ of Latter Day Saints. Members of the church are commonly known as Mormons. Savannah, who is identified only by her first name, was twelve years old when she came out to her Mormon family as a lesbian. Savannah decided that she wanted to share this part of her identity with her community. In 2017, she spoke about her sexuality and identity at a religious gathering. "I do believe [God] made me this way on purpose," Savannah said. "No part of me is a mistake."[24] After a few minutes, church leaders cut off her microphone and asked her to return to her seat. As of 2016, the Mormon church recognizes that same-sex attractions are not a choice and does not condemn them as sinful. But the church believes that acting on attractions to people of the same sex is a sin. The church does not recognize same-sex marriage and does not allow openly LGBT people to become ordained members of the church. Although Savannah's words were silenced, she does not regret her actions. "There's been a lot of homicides or deaths," because of LGBT intolerance, Savannah told reporters. "I wanted some change."[25] On April 4, 2019, the Mormon church lifted a rule that had prevented children of LGBT couples from being baptized into the church.

> **"I do believe [God] made me this way on purpose. No part of me is a mistake."** [24]
>
> —Savannah, a lesbian Mormon teen

LGBT people who want to stay connected with their cultural heritage can face similar barriers. Many cultures are heteronormative. For example, Saint Patrick's Day is a cultural holiday for Americans to celebrate Irish heritage. Many cities with Irish American communities host Saint Patrick's Day parades where people can gather and celebrate. However, there are examples of these parades discriminating against the LGBT community. The Pride Center of Staten Island, an LGBT resource center in New York, has been denied a spot in the Staten Island Saint Patrick's Day Parade since 2011. The executive director of the Pride Center was not even allowed to apply to march, a decision she told reporters "screams discrimination."[26] The larger New York City parade only began allowing LGBT groups to march in 2016. In 2017, organizers of the Saint Patrick's Day parade in Boston, Massachusetts, decided to ban an LGBT veterans' group from marching. After public pressure, including from the city's mayor, the parade organizers changed their decision.

LGBT DISCRIMINATION IN MEDIA AND PUBLIC LIFE

The media landscape changed drastically for LGBT people throughout the end of the twentieth century and the beginning of the twenty-first century. As of 2018, Ellen DeGeneres, an openly gay woman, was one of the richest and most successful people in Hollywood. She has a net worth of about $400 million, in large part due to her talk show, *The Ellen DeGeneres Show*, which has been on the air since 2003. She is married to a woman, model and actor Portia de Rossi. In 1997, however, DeGeneres was the closeted star of her own sitcom. That year, DeGeneres came out to the world with a *Time* magazine cover and, as her character Ellen Morgan, came out on TV as the first openly LGBT sitcom lead. DeGeneres remembers that she was tired of keeping a secret she wasn't ashamed of. "It made it look like something was wrong," she said.[27] DeGeneres's coming out caused a national sensation, and she received angry messages and death threats as well as praise. In the decades since DeGeneres's coming out, it has become far more common for public figures to be open about their sexuality. In 2014, Apple CEO Tim Cook became the first

Ellen DeGeneres poses for a photo at the People's Choice Awards in 2015. DeGeneres, a famous TV personality, publicly came out as gay in 1997.

head of a major company to come out as gay. Still, in some cases, openly declaring an LGBT identity is a career risk for public figures. Also in 2014, football player Michael Sam made history as the first openly gay player to be drafted to a National Football League (NFL) team. However, Sam believes that his decision to be open about his sexuality cost him his professional career. He retired in 2015 after having trouble making any team's final roster. "I think if I never would have came out . . . I would still be currently in the NFL," Sam told a journalist.[28]

The media also plays a large role in shaping public perceptions of the LGBT community. In many cases, popular media such as songs,

"BURY YOUR GAYS"

Tropes are common storylines, symbols, or themes, with meanings that are well-known and understood in society. Popular media such as movies, books, and TV shows are full of tropes, ideas and events that show up in many different stories. One common trope in contemporary American culture is something critics have labeled "Bury Your Gays." The phrase refers to the tendency of fictional LGBT characters to die more often than their straight counterparts. In 2016, the LGBT women's website *Autostraddle* compiled a list of more than 200 lesbian and bisexual TV characters who had been killed off of their shows. In a TV landscape with very few LGBT female characters, 200 is a striking number of deaths.

These characters' deaths aren't real, but LGBT characters' increased likelihood of death sends a message. According to the website *TV Tropes*, which analyzes and collects popular cultural tropes, the "Bury Your Gays" trope helps send the message that LGBT lives are less important than straight ones or that living as an LGBT person is inherently dangerous or scary. It's true that in real life, LGBT people are more vulnerable to some forms of violence. However, observers point out that the "Bury Your Gays" trope can reinforce the false belief that, in the words of *TV Tropes*, "gay characters just aren't allowed happy endings."

"Analysis/Bury Your Gays," TV Tropes, *n.d. www.tvtropes.org.*

movies, and TV shows help perpetuate negative stereotypes about LGBT people. One example comes from the world of Disney movies. Disney's animated films may be aimed at children, but most have an evil villain that the viewer is meant to root against. In many cases, this villain shares many personality traits with an LGBT stereotype. The evil Queen Ursula from the Disney version of *The Little Mermaid* was based on a drag performer named Divine. "Films need villains, and for a very long time, the effete, aristocratic, effeminate man was the villain," journalist David Thorpe said in an interview with *Vice*.[29]

Thorpe means that gay men are often stereotyped as feminine, snobby, and mean. Thorpe points to the evil Jafar, from Disney's *Aladdin*, as another take on this stereotype. Jafar is snobby, sarcastic, and fancily dressed. In the movie, these attributes are signs of his evil nature—but they are also negative personality traits associated with the stereotype of a feminine gay man. When villains in children's stories are given these stereotypical characteristics, it sends a message about how LGBT identity is viewed as a "threat to the moral order," according to Thorpe, and as something that stands in the way of a goal such as marriage between a male and female character.[30] Thorpe is not against having some storybook villains be gay, but he says he wants to see artists go beyond lazy and demeaning stereotypes when creating characters.

LGBT DISCRIMINATION IN HEALTH CARE

Legally married couples have the ability to visit sick partners in the hospital and take part in important health-care decisions in cases of emergency. But same-sex couples have not always enjoyed these rights. In the past, before same-sex marriage was legalized, it was common for same-sex partners of sick patients to be blocked from visiting their loved ones in the hospital. In 2011, the US government started requiring all hospitals that received federal Medicaid and Medicare funding to not discriminate against LGBT people in their visitation rules. This meant most hospitals were required to allow same-sex partner visits. The legalization of same-sex marriage later strengthened same-sex families' ability to visit with sick partners and make decisions about critical care.

Nevertheless, many LGBT people still report discrimination and bias within the health-care system. Research by the Human

Rights Campaign shows that most LGBT people have experienced discrimination within the US health-care system. Transgender people are especially likely to experience discrimination, with many dreading encounters with transphobic medical staff. Human Rights Campaign research found that 73 percent of trans people reported that they believe they will be treated differently by health-care providers because of their identity. One transgender man, who remained anonymous, reported, "After learning I was born female, the doctor kept calling me 'she' in front of all the staff and other patients, no matter how many times I corrected him."[31] For transgender people who undergo medical transition, prejudice and intolerance in the health-care system is a heavy burden.

"After learning I was born female, the doctor kept calling me 'she' in front of all the staff and other patients, no matter how many times I corrected him." [31]

—*A transgender man in the US health-care system*

HOW DOES
INTOLERANCE HURT
LGBT PEOPLE?

Discrimination against LGBT people has widespread and lasting effects. One of the most immediate dangers of LGBT intolerance is physical harm. People live with the risk of being attacked or murdered just for identifying as LGBT. Anti-LGBT bias also affects people's ability to meet basic needs for shelter and employment. Homelessness is especially common among young LGBT people. LGBT intolerance is also a health risk, as the stresses of anti-LGBT bias increase the risk of certain mental illnesses and health conditions. And LGBT intolerance can even take deep root in the hearts and minds of LGBT people, making it difficult for them to accept themselves.

VIOLENCE AGAINST LGBT PEOPLE

LGBT people are at risk for hate crimes and violence. According to 2009 research, one in five members of the LGBT community had been the victim of a crime motivated by their sexual and gender identity. According to a national survey of LGBT people, approximately 13 percent were victims of a violent crime at some point in their lives.

Some members of the LGBT community are more vulnerable to violence than others. For instance, people of color who identify as LGBT face racism as well as homophobia or transphobia, and the

People gather at a vigil to remember the victims of a mass shooting at Pulse, an LGBT nightclub in Orlando, Florida, in 2016. Forty-nine people were killed and many others were injured in one of the deadliest shootings in US history, an attack on the LGBT community.

combination of these oppressions can make their lives especially dangerous. A 2014 Human Rights Campaign report found that black victims of anti-LGBT attacks were more likely than other victims to experience physical harm and to be harmed by police. Columnist Clay Cane once spoke to his best friend, a fellow black gay man, about an assault he experienced in his early twenties. Cane's friend was attacked by two men while others looked on and didn't help. He never reported the attack to police, assuming that they also would not care about the violence he experienced.

Trans women of color, who face sexism, racism, and transphobia, are especially vulnerable to violence. Additionally, American trans women of color are at high risk for poverty and homelessness, in part because of widespread discrimination in the job market and in their social lives. Partly because of employment discrimination, trans women of color are more likely than others to illegally work as sex workers to financially support themselves. But illegal industries lack official job protections and regulations. This means that trans women of color, already at increased risk for violence, face additional risks within the illegal sex industry.

In 2018, at least twenty-two transgender people were murdered in the United States. At least 128 transgender people have been murdered in the United States since 2013. Most of these were transgender women of color. Transgender women of color are also at an elevated risk of HIV. The US Centers for Disease Control and Prevention (CDC) estimates approximately 25 percent of all American trans women and 56 percent of black American trans women are living with HIV. As transgender women are vulnerable to physical violence, poverty, homelessness, and life-threatening HIV, the average life expectancy of a trans woman of color is just thirty-five years.

Ashlee Marie Preston is a black transgender woman and the first openly transgender person to head a magazine, *Wear Your Voice*. Preston left home at nineteen years old to find trans community. She was homeless and used drugs during parts of her young adulthood. Today, Preston advocates on behalf of other trans women of color. In June 2018, Preston celebrated her thirty-fourth birthday with a cake decorated in memory of murdered black trans women. The cake read, "Today, I turn 34. Statistically, I won't live over 35. Black trans women will no longer accept this."[32] Preston decided to start a social media hashtag, #ThriveOver35. The hashtag is devoted to creating safe spaces for trans women of color and educating others about the dangers trans women face. In an online video, Preston publicly shared her goals for herself and other black trans women. "We need

to talk about economic opportunities for black trans women . . . mental health, trauma," Preston said. "It's important that we utilize social media as an opportunity to tell our stories."[33]

Trans people are also at special risk in the US prison system. Sixteen percent of American trans people

"Today, I turn 34. Statistically, I won't live over 35. Black trans women will no longer accept this.**"** [32]

—Ashlee Marie Preston, activist and black transgender woman

have been incarcerated, a proportion that is more than five times higher than that of the general population. Almost half of all black trans women have been to prison. There are some regulations requiring officials to take people's gender identities into account when assigning them to prisons, but most transgender women inmates are held in men's prisons. Trans women who are forced to identify as men in prison suffer from the psychological and physical effects of gender dysphoria, which is the stress caused by having a body and societal expectations of gender that do not match one's own gender identity. According to the National Center for Transgender Equality, trans women are also at especially high risk for sexual assault in prison. Strawberry Hampton, a trans woman serving a prison sentence for burglary, was initially assigned to a men's prison. She was forced to cut her hair and trim her nails and was bullied by inmates and guards. She said these experiences made her feel "inhuman."[34] In 2018, Hampton successfully lobbied for a transfer to a women's prison.

HOMELESSNESS AND LGBT YOUTH

Young LGBT people are at an increased risk of homelessness. Young people are sometimes kicked out of their homes by parents or family members who do not accept their sexual or gender identities.

This means they are more likely to end up living in homeless shelters or on the streets. Young LGBT people make up about 20 to 40 percent of homeless young people. And being homeless is dangerous—53 percent of homeless LGBT youth report being sexually assaulted, and more than 60 percent have attempted suicide at least once. Frankie is a transgender person younger than twenty.

In an interview with photographer Letizia Mariotti, Frankie described ending up without a place to call home: "My parents tried to ignore what they called 'my lifestyle' and pretended that it would go away. . . . The tension at home just kept rising until one day my mom . . . told me to leave and not come back."[35] Frankie struggled to find food and shelter, working as a sex worker and having dangerous encounters with customers. "You have no security," Frankie remembers, "and you can only keep what you can hold in a bag or suitcase."[36]

> "My parents tried to ignore what they called 'my lifestyle' and pretended that it would go away."[35]
>
> —Frankie, a transgender person

HEALTH EFFECTS OF LGBT INTOLERANCE

Discrimination in the health-care system takes a toll on the health of the LGBT community. In North America, the HIV/AIDS epidemic has lessened greatly since the 1980s. However, LGBT Americans are still disproportionately affected by the disease. As of 2017, about 1.2 million Americans were living with HIV, the infection that can develop into the AIDS virus. A little more than half of those infected are gay and bisexual men. As of 2009, almost one-third of transgender

Americans were infected with HIV. HIV infection is especially prevalent among African American LGBT people. Fifty-six percent of African American trans women are HIV positive, and 38 percent of gay and bisexual men infected with HIV are African American.

There are effective medications for treating and preventing HIV, such as antiretroviral medications, which can increase a patient's life expectancy by almost forty years. However, as of 2015, only 39 percent of infected Americans had seen a doctor specializing in HIV, and only 30 percent were taking drugs that could effectively control their HIV. There is a medical drug called Truvada that reduces the risk of contracting HIV through sex. The practice of taking a drug like Truvada in attempt to reduce a risk for HIV is called pre-exposure prophylaxis (PrEP). People who do PrEP daily are 90 percent less likely to contract HIV through sex, research shows. However, many at-risk people do not know about Truvada or are not using the drug. As of 2014, research showed that only 26 percent of American gay men knew about Truvada. In March 2019, only about 20 percent of people who could benefit from PrEP were taking Truvada. This is partly because Truvada and PrEP have not always been well publicized and are difficult to access in some areas of the United States. In addition, some people argue against PrEP, saying it may be unsafely encouraging gay men to have sex without the protection of condoms.

Some of the stresses specific to the LGBT community—from family exclusion to discrimination—increase vulnerability to mental illnesses. LGBT people are at higher risk of depression, anxiety, and substance abuse. According to the National Alliance on Mental Illness, LGBT people are "almost 3 times more likely than others to experience a mental health condition such as major depression or generalized

People remember those who died at the height of the AIDS epidemic in many ways. In 2011, New York residents Christopher Tepper and Paul Kelterborn started advocating for a memorial that would commemorate the lives of more than 100,000 New Yorkers who lost their lives to AIDS. On World AIDS Day, December 1, 2016, the New York AIDS Memorial was unveiled to the public for the first time. The memorial, a white triangular structure on a small plot of land, is located near the historic headquarters of ACT UP, Gay Men's Health Crisis, and other groups that fought AIDS in the early years of the crisis. In San Francisco, the National AIDS Memorial Grove contains the names of thousands of AIDS victims. They are etched into the stones and pathways inside the grove. The AIDS memorial quilt began in 1987 as a collaboration between the friends and loved ones of people who had died of AIDS. The organizers invited people to contribute a three-by-six-foot (0.9 m by 1.8 m) cloth panel that paid tribute to a person who had died of AIDS. More than 48,000 of these panels combined into a single quilt. Portions of the quilt tour the country so that viewers can learn about those who lost their lives to AIDS. On Instagram, an account with the username theaidsmemorial has posted more than 5,000 photos and remembrances of people who died from the disease.

anxiety disorder."[37] LGBT people report higher rates of drug use than straight people. They abuse alcohol at rates more than twice that of the general population. Within the LGBT community, bisexual people are at especially high risk of mental illness.

Rufus Wainwright is an openly gay musician and composer. When he was young, he began using illegal drugs such as crystal meth, an addictive stimulant that causes intense feelings of pleasure and bursts of energy. Wainwright was drawn to the drug in part to escape the effects of the discrimination he felt in daily life. "Years of sexual insecurity, the low-grade discrimination you suffer, the need to belong—[crystal meth] takes care of all that in one second,"

Wainwright recalled in an interview.[38] Wainwright was addicted to the drug for several years and abused other substances as well. He is thankful he managed to enter a rehabilitation program before suffering lasting damage to his health.

According to the National Eating Disorders Association, members of the LGBT community are at a high risk for developing eating disorders. Discrimination, bullying, and violence all increase a person's vulnerability to eating disorders. For some transgender people, gender dysphoria can increase the risk of developing an eating disorder. A transgender man who identified himself by his first name, Adam, talked to *Marie Claire* magazine about suffering from an eating disorder in his teens. "I was so disgusted with my form and the gender dissonance it inspired," Adam remembers. "I was pudgy, oily, and growing breasts that I loathed."[39] Adam began dieting dangerously and exercising obsessively until he developed serious complications and had to be hospitalized. At the lowest point of his illness, his body lost the ability to control its temperature properly.

Members of the LGBT community are also more likely to attempt suicide than straight, cisgender people. According to a CDC study, LGBT teens are three times more likely than straight teens to seriously consider suicide. More than one-quarter of transgender youth report having attempted suicide at some point in their lives. In order to address this crisis, one nonprofit, the Trevor Project, offers a 24/7 crisis hotline through phone, text, and instant messaging for LGBT people younger than twenty-five who are considering suicide.

BARRIERS TO TRANSITION

People also generally face intolerance and other barriers in the process of transitioning genders. Transgender people decide to

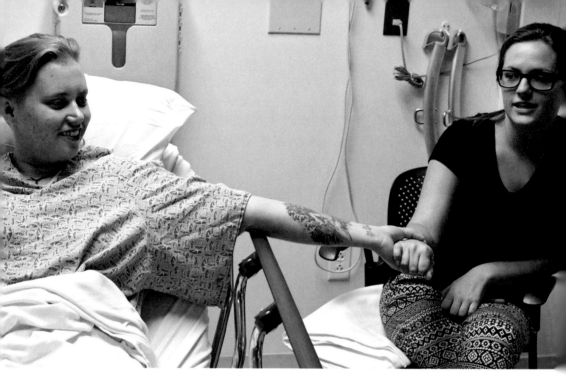

EJ Silverberg, a transgender man, holds his girlfriend's hand after undergoing surgery to have his breasts removed at a hospital in Boston, Massachusetts. Silverberg has publicly shared the story of his transition with the hope that it will help others.

transition in many ways. Many trans people begin a public transition with steps such as changing their name, clothing, and hairstyle to reflect their gender identity. These steps are known as social transition. Some transgender people choose only to transition socially. Others also pursue steps such as hormone therapy and surgeries to live out their gender identities. This is called medical transition.

Medical transition is a complex and expensive process. People who wish to undergo hormone therapy and/or sex reassignment surgery typically work with psychiatrists, pharmacists, primary care professionals, and other health-care workers. Transition may involve multiple surgeries, each costing thousands of dollars. Many transgender people cannot get insurance coverage for transition, and it is common for transgender people to try to raise money in other ways. As of 2018, President Donald Trump's administration had planned to cut back regulations that protect transgender people from health-care discrimination and keep health insurers from limiting coverage of medical transition procedures.

Writer Daniel Ortberg transitioned to male in his early thirties. As part of his transition, he chose to remove his breast tissue to make his torso appear more masculine. The surgery cost $6,250 and was not covered by insurance. In an essay, Ortberg reflected on the expenses and hurdles he and other trans people have faced in getting surgery: "I had friends who thought their surgery was going to be covered by their insurance company right up until the day itself, and friends whose claims were denied after the fact; I knew people whose fundraisers never made a big enough splash to even cover the cost of their pre- and post-op prescriptions; someone whose surgeon said at the last minute, just as they were going under, 'I know we talked about [Technique X] but I'm going to go with [Technique Y].'"[40] Ortberg has no regrets about his surgery, calling it "the best money [he's] ever spent."[41] But even with the ability to pay for expensive procedures, arranging for other medical elements of transitioning, such as hormones, is expensive and exhausting. Ortberg takes the hormone testosterone, which helps the body develop traditionally male characteristics such as facial hair. He has shared his difficulties in getting his prescription refilled, including pharmacists who address him by the wrong name or claim to be confused by his medication requests. "I get [testosterone] in five-month stocks, and it takes me the full five months to get my refills approved," Ortberg shared on Twitter.[42]

INTERNALIZED HOMOPHOBIA AND TRANSPHOBIA

Along with everyone else in American society, members of the LGBT community grow up absorbing stereotypical messages about being LGBT. As a result, many LGBT people struggle with internalized homophobia and/or internalized transphobia. Homophobia is the hatred of or prejudice against lesbian, gay, and bisexual people, and transphobia is anti-transgender feeling and bias. Internalized homophobia and transphobia occur when LGBT people apply the intolerant messages of their surrounding culture to their own self-images. These internalized feelings of self-hate can make it difficult for LGBT people to truly love and accept themselves and form strong relationships with others in the LGBT community.

One way that internalized homophobia manifests is in some lesbian, gay, and bisexual people's desire not to seem gay to others. Lesbian, gay, and bisexual people may want to distance themselves from harmful stereotypes by putting down stereotypically lesbian, gay, and bisexual interests or behaviors or by taking pride in appearing straight to others. Writer and humorist David Sedaris has been openly gay for most of his adult life. In a documentary interview, Sedaris talked about the complicated feelings he experiences when someone doesn't realize that he is gay. "It's like, why does that make me feel good?" Sedaris said. "And I hate myself for thinking that."[43] For other LGBT people, internalized self-hate can delay their process of coming out. The actress Amandla Stenberg came out as bisexual in her mid-teens, but she felt she was still hiding the truth of her identity. Although she did not feel comfortable in relationships with men, Stenberg was not yet ready to identify as a lesbian. In 2018, at age nineteen, Stenberg clarified that she identified not only as queer but also as a lesbian. Stenberg said in an interview that internalized homophobia had delayed her acknowledgement of the truth. "I was scared—on a personal and public level—to confront what I was," she said.[44]

THE GLASS CLOSET

In 1978, Marilyn Loden coined a phrase to describe her sense of an invisible, unspoken force that kept women from ascending to the highest levels of leadership. She called it *the glass ceiling*. People now commonly use this phrase to refer to the societal sexism that makes it challenging for women to advance professionally. In a similar sense, some people have used the phrase *the glass closet* to describe the societal expectation that LGBT people should stay silent about their sexuality in order to appear respectable and mainstream. Under this expectation, people do not necessarily have to pretend to be straight, but they cannot honestly and openly discuss their sexual orientation, either. One example of a celebrity who was considered to be in the glass closet is TV journalist Anderson Cooper. Cooper, who is gay, began his journalism career in 1992. For twenty years, he neither confirmed nor denied his sexuality publicly. Still, Cooper was not able to avoid intense media focus on his sexuality, subjecting him to constant rumors and speculation about his relationships. Cooper publicly came out in 2012.

For transgender people, internalized transphobia can show up as a punishing self-image. In a personal blog post, Rachel Williams, a transgender woman, discusses how internalized transphobia had kept her from accepting her appearance. Although she is proud of her body and her looks, which don't necessarily resemble those of a cisgender woman, Williams has sometimes found herself thinking that she was not a stereotypically "real" woman. She catches herself occasionally eyeing other trans women critically, evaluating them to see if they could pass as having been born female. Williams believes that internalized transphobia is unavoidable in an intolerant culture. However, she argues for an end to transphobic self-judgment. "We need to reject the idea that the ONLY women are women who embody [cisgender body standards]," Williams writes.[45]

CHAPTER
FOUR

WHAT IS THE FUTURE OF GENDER AND SEXUAL EQUALITY?

The word *queer* used to be considered an offensive slur against LGBT people. But the LGBT community has worked to reclaim that term, and today, many LGBT people embrace *queer* as a term of unity and pride. In a 2017 interview, musician Ellen Kempner talked about how she felt connected to people of different LGBT identities. "I am proud to be queer and embrace my own identity, but what really makes my chest swell is feeling a part of a greater association," Kempner told *Billboard* magazine.[46] The reclamation of the term *queer* is just one example of the immense progress the LGBT community has made over the past century. The LGBT community will likely continue to include shifting understandings of gender and sexuality in the future. However, LGBT people will also probably continue to face intolerance, including cultural and legal challenges.

BEYOND THE GENDER BINARY

A growing number of people do not identify as either male or female. Nonbinary gender identities are identities other than the two options of man or woman. People with nonbinary identities may choose to use personal pronouns other than *he* and *him* or *she* and *her*. *They* and

Members of the LGBT community and their allies have worked to promote tolerance and inclusion. However, LGBT people still face discrimination and challenges.

them are a common pronoun choice for nonbinary people. Nonbinary people may also identify as being agender, which means having no gender at all, or as demigender, identifying only somewhat with manhood or womanhood. Others may identify with more than one gender or with different genders at different times.

People who identify as nonbinary can have a wide variety of gender expressions. Sam Escobar is a young nonbinary person who was assigned female at birth. Most strangers still perceive Escobar as a woman. In an article for *Esquire* magazine, Escobar, who uses the personal pronoun *they*, reflected on what it was like to be a trans person who did not undergo a medical transition and what nonbinary identity means to them. Escobar first decided to explore their nonbinary identity by dressing in men's clothing and using a garment called a binder to minimize the appearance of their breasts. But though Escobar didn't identify as female, this androgynous identity didn't feel right to them either. Finally, Escobar remembers, "I experienced an important self-discovery: I don't need to look a certain way to identify, and to feel, the way that I do."[47] Today, Escobar is out as nonbinary to their social circle and feels lucky that they are "able to count on the support system I've built around me to accept me as I am."[48]

> "I experienced an important self-discovery: I don't need to look a certain way to identify, and to feel, the way that I do."[47]
>
> —Sam Escobar, on their nonbinary gender identity

Wider understanding and acceptance of nonbinary identities have led some people to embrace them later in life. Masha Gessen is a writer and journalist who was born in Russia in the 1960s. Gessen spent years identifying as a lesbian woman, but, "now that I'm in my fifties and younger people have made up a name for it," Gessen writes, "I call myself nonbinary."[49] Gessen feels exhausted after a lifetime of being questioned about gender. Gessen wishes for a world in which gender is not constantly recorded, where official documents and public restrooms would not require people to specify their sex.

INTERSEX IDENTITY AND EXPERIENCE

Not everyone is assigned female or male gender at birth. As many as 2 percent of people have bodies that differ from those traditionally associated with either male or female. About one in 2,000 babies is born with a combination of male and female traits. These people are considered intersex rather than male or female. Since the 1950s, it has been standard practice in the United States to have parents choose a gender, either male or female, for very young intersex children based on the child's outward appearance and the advice of clinicians, rather than simply raising the child to identify as intersex. Today, medical treatments for intersex children vary, but the Intersex Society of North America believes that it is still common for medical professionals to choose one gender on a young intersex child's behalf, concealing the child's intersex identity. In many cases, parents choose to give intersex babies and children medically unnecessary surgeries to give their bodies a more traditionally male or female appearance. These surgeries can have harmful physical and psychological effects. Advocates are pushing to stop this process in favor of medical treatment that has the intersex person's full consent.

Kimberly Mascott Zieselman is an intersex person and the director of InterACT, an organization that advocates for the needs of young intersex people. When Zieselman was a teenager, surgeons conducted a genital removal surgery without her consent. "It's time for these surgeries to stop," Zieselman says.[50] In 2018, InterACT helped pass a California resolution against unnecessary surgery on intersex children.

Some governments are choosing to change the way they record gender on official documents. In June 2017, Oregon passed a law to let residents identify as a third gender on their driver's licenses. Washington, DC, Washington state, and New York have similar laws. As of January 2019, a law allows New York City residents who do not identify as either male or female to amend their birth certificates to an "X" gender identity. California law allows residents to change their gender to nonbinary on all legal documents. These places join several countries that allow citizens to identify as a gender other than male or female. As of September 2018, Bangladesh, India, Pakistan, Nepal, Malta, Australia, New Zealand, Canada, Germany, and Denmark all offered third gender options on some official documents, such as birth certificates or passports.

Some nonbinary people celebrate the opportunity to have their identities officially recognized. Davi, a nonbinary person living in California, told the website *Vox*, "As soon as I am able to change my documents to match my name and gender identity, I will, and I will be so grateful and less tired once this all happens." Other people would prefer to have a legal system that doesn't depend so much on identifying gender. "Gender should be removed entirely from all IDs," a queer trans person named Mya told *Vox*.

Quoted in Annie Tritt, "States are Starting to Recognize a Third Gender. Here's What That Means for Nonbinary Youth," Vox, April 2, 2018. www.vox.com.

THE LGBTQIA+ UMBRELLA

There are many different iterations of the acronym *LGBT*. It is commonly written as *LGBTQ* to include people who identify as queer or questioning. In more recent years, the acronym has been expanded to include nonbinary people and intersex people as well. Some people now prefer to use *LGBTQIA+* instead of either *LGBT* or *LGBTQ*. The *I* in this acronym refers to intersex identity, and the *A* is for people who identify as asexual. Asexual people feel little or no sexual desire for other people. Some people say the *A* can also stand for *allies*, referring to people who do not identify as sexual or gender minorities but support those who do. However, many LGBT advocates argue that while allies are appreciated, they should not be included in the acronym because being an ally is a chosen action, not an identity. The plus sign (+) sometimes added is meant to embrace other identities not mentioned in the acronym. For example, some people identify not as gay, lesbian, or bisexual but as pansexual, attracted to people of all gender and sexual identities. The collection of these terms and the various versions of the acronym are known collectively as the LGBTQIA umbrella. The acronym may continue to grow as society embraces more and more gender and sexual identities.

REPRESENTATION AND FIGHTING STEREOTYPES

LGBT Americans are finding more opportunities to represent their community publicly. Public representation is important, because it will allow young LGBT people to grow up seeing themselves better reflected in the world around them. In November 2018, more openly LGBT politicians were elected to political office than at any other time in US history. At least 153 LGBT candidates won congressional, gubernatorial, and state legislature elections across the country. This group included Kyrsten Sinema, a Democratic senator from Arizona who is the first openly bisexual senator in US history. Before being elected to the Senate, Sinema served for six years in the House of Representatives, where she was the first and only openly bisexual member of Congress. Kansas Democrat Sharice Davids was also among those elected in November 2018, becoming the first openly LGBT Kansan to serve in Congress, as well as one of the first two

US Representative Sharice Davids, a Democrat from Kansas, is the first openly LGBT Native American to serve in Congress. She has advocated for women, people of color, veterans, and the LGBT community.

Native American women elected to the House. Davids is passionate about using her experiences as a gay Native American woman and a first-generation college student to represent other Americans. "Native Americans, gay people, the unemployed and the underemployed have to fight like hell just to survive," Davids said during her campaign.[51]

There are also people leading the way to greater representation and inclusion in entertainment and popular media. In 1985, a group of activists formed the group GLAAD to protest biased media coverage of the HIV/AIDS epidemic. Since then, GLAAD has worked to monitor discriminatory representations of LGBT people in the media and promote positive, accurate media narratives. The landscape of LGBT media representation has improved. One example comes from the world of children's TV. *Steven Universe* is a cartoon TV series that follows the life of Steven, a half-human, half–Crystal Gem raised by magical Crystal Gems who help guard the universe. In July 2018, *Steven Universe* became the first children's show to feature a marriage proposal between two women. The show includes multiple characters who identify as LGBT or do not follow traditional gender norms, celebrating them as heroes. While the show's open celebration of LGBT characters has been controversial at times—one episode was censored in the United Kingdom for featuring a same-sex kiss—many fans say *Steven Universe* sends a positive message to LGBT children and youth. As a fan wrote in a petition supporting the show, "*Steven Universe* gave me the courage to embrace who I really am. . . . Queer kids deserve representation."[52]

MAKING NEW TRADITIONS

In 1991, the average age of an LGBT person coming out for the first time was twenty-five. By 2011, that average age had dropped to sixteen. A 2013 survey found that more than 90 percent of LGBT Americans thought that society was more accepting of the LGBT community than it had been ten years earlier. As more people feel safe and fulfilled living openly as LGBT, traditions for celebrating and commemorating LGBT life milestones continue to grow and change.

Across the world, June is LGBT Pride month. The month of June was chosen to commemorate the anniversary of the Stonewall Uprising. During Pride month, cities and towns worldwide hold Pride

The famous rainbow LGBT pride flag was designed in 1978. It has become an iconic symbol for the LGBT community.

parades and celebrations as well as workshops and commemorative events. Some Pride parades draw millions of people. In 2018, the Brazilian city of São Paolo hosted the biggest Pride parade in history, with more than 3 million people having fun and making their voices heard. Many Pride celebrations feature the rainbow flag of LGBT pride. Gilbert Baker, a designer, came up with the idea for the flag in 1978 after his friend Harvey Milk asked him to design a symbol for the LGBT community. Baker was inspired by the fights for gay rights going on around him at the time. "This was our new revolution: a tribal, individualistic, and collective vision. It deserved a new symbol," Baker wrote.[53] He created a flag that would have "its own idea of power," he said.[54] The rainbow flag has bright-colored stripes. It has become an indelible symbol uniting the LGBT community.

As more LGBT people feel comfortable coming out, rituals for sharing their identities with family and friends are evolving. Many people turn to social media sites such as Twitter, Instagram, and Facebook to help them come out. In 2013, a fifteen-year-old girl identified as Laurel came out to her family with a cake that read "I'm gay" in icing and a note filled with cake-related puns. "I hope you still love me . . . your acceptance would be the icing on the cake," Laurel wrote.[55] Laurel told the *Huffington Post* that her family had welcomed her news. Since 1988, October 11 has been National Coming Out Day, a holiday to celebrate being out as LGBT and to offer people a chance to come out.

Jordan Reeves grew up in a small town where it was difficult to connect with other LGBT people. After coming out at age twenty-three, Reeves wanted a place online where other people could share their stories. He created VideoOut as a video library for LGBTQIA+ people to share their coming out stories. VideoOut's goal is to provide coming out stories that inspire the next generation of LGBT youth. "We believe that one story is important, several stories are powerful, and all of our stories together are an unstoppable force," Reeves says.[56]

Ideas about what it means to come out have changed and evolved as well. Elijah Nealy, a professor and social worker who mentors trans youth, points out that for trans people, the coming out process is ongoing. "There is never a time when trans people will 'finish' coming out," Nealy says.[57] As trans people meet new people and move through new stages of life, they must make decisions about who to talk with about their trans identity. Many lesbian, gay, and bisexual people echo the sentiment that coming out is an always ongoing process, not an event. Figure skater Adam Rippon, who is gay, says coming out is "about finding out who you are in stages, through moments of self-discovery."[58]

LGBT INTOLERANCE IN US LEGISLATION

The United States military has a long history of excluding and discriminating against LGBT people. Throughout the twentieth century, several laws and policies allowed the military to discharge people who identified as gay or had same-sex experiences, and people who openly identified as gay, lesbian, or bisexual were not allowed to serve. In 1993, President Bill Clinton's administration introduced a policy called Don't Ask, Don't Tell, in which lesbian, gay, and bisexual people were allowed to serve in the military as long as they did not discuss their sexual orientation openly. In 2001 alone, more than 1,200 people were discharged from the military over Don't Ask, Don't Tell violations. In July 2011, Don't Ask, Don't Tell was repealed, allowing lesbian, gay, and bisexual people to serve openly in the US military for the first time. In 2016, President Barack Obama's administration extended this right to trans people. The military employs more American transgender people than any other organization. However, in 2017, President Donald Trump announced a policy that would ban all transgender people "who require or have undergone gender transition" from military service.[59] Previously, transgender people had been allowed to serve in the military and get funding for sex reassignment surgery. As part of his reasoning behind the ban, Trump claimed on Twitter that medical costs associated with transgender military members were too high and that their presence was disruptive. In January 2019, the Supreme Court upheld Trump's ban. Lawyers challenging the policy wrote, "The government has presented no evidence that [trans people serving in the military] harms military readiness, effectiveness or lethality."[60] Jody Davis, a transgender woman, talked to the *New York Times* about her disappointment with the decision. Davis had already served in the military for eight years, but under Trump's policy, she would not be able to do so again. "It's ironic," Davis said. "I've already proved myself, and now they say I'm disqualified."[61]

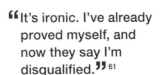

"It's ironic. I've already proved myself, and now they say I'm disqualified." [61]

—*Jody Davis, a transgender woman who had hoped to rejoin the US military before the 2019 ban was upheld*

There are also many state government bills and policies that discriminate against LGBT people. As of November 2018, the Victory Fund, a national organization that works to elect LGBT leaders, had tracked more than 300 anti-LGBT bills and proposals. Among these proposed laws was a 2019 Utah bill seeking to prevent people in that state from changing the sex on their birth certificates. In 2018, Oklahoma and Kansas both passed laws that would allow foster and adoption agencies to avoid placing children with LGBT couples.

GLOBAL STRUGGLES FOR LGBT RIGHTS

In 2015, the United States became the nineteenth country to legalize same-sex marriage. As of July 2018, twenty-seven countries gave full marriage rights to same-sex couples. However, approximately

SEX REASSIGNMENT AND STERILIZATION

In 1972, the country of Sweden updated its laws to allow transgender people to officially change their sex. The change came with a requirement, however. People who wished to legally change their sex had to also agree to be sterilized. Sterilization is the act of making someone unable to have children. Through medical procedures, doctors can block the paths of eggs and sperm so that a person is unable to reproduce. But forced sterilization is not medically necessary and takes away transgender people's reproductive rights. Sweden's sterilization requirement came from a belief that transgender people were not fit to be parents. Sweden ended its sterilization requirement for trans people in 2013. However, until a 2017 European Court of Human Rights decision, twenty European countries still required transgender people to be sterilized. As of 2017, Slovenia, Bosnia and Herzegovina, Serbia, Montenegro, and Turkey all had sterilization laws.

Sterilization of transgender people is not only a problem in Europe. As of 2018, Japanese trans people were required to be single and have no children younger than twenty in order to medically transition. They were also required to undergo sterilization so they could not have biological children after transitioning. These legal requirements have been challenged in court, but Japan's Supreme Court upheld the law in early 2019.

40 percent of countries criminalized homosexuality as of 2018. There are some countries in which killing people for engaging in same-sex intimacy is either legal or commonly accepted. Most countries in the world do not legally allow same-sex couples to adopt children. And, just as in the United States, in most parts of the world LGBT people face a complex mix of legal and cultural barriers to inclusion.

In Russia, for example, sex acts between people of the same sex are not penalized. However, a 2013 law makes it illegal for citizens to create "propaganda of non-traditional sexual relations among minors."[62] In practice, this means that Russians can be convicted for offering sex education to LGBT youth. In Chechnya, an autonomous republic within Russian control, local authorities have been rounding up and executing groups of LGBT people. LGBT Chechens fear torture and executions. In January 2017, twenty-seven men were collected in one night and killed under the reasoning that they were suspected terrorists. A lesbian woman named Marko told reporters that she fled Chechnya after her own family threatened to kill or torture her. A gay man who goes by the name Ruslan knew of other people who had been kidnapped or disappeared. "Some were caught . . . and beaten violently. Some were never found: their relatives didn't even bother looking for them," Ruslan told a news reporter.[63] Despite widespread reports of anti-gay attacks, the Chechen government denies any wrongdoing. As of 2018, dozens of LGBT Chechens had fled the country in attempt to find safety in other parts of the world. The Human Rights Campaign has asked the United States government to welcome Chechen residents and other asylum seekers fleeing homophobic or transphobic violence.

LGBT AWARENESS AND EDUCATION

There are several organizations working to educate people on LGBT issues. The TransActive Gender Center is based in Portland, Oregon. Since 2007, it has offered workshops and seminars on supporting trans people, including training sessions on gender diversity, trans history, supporting trans kids, and trans rights. The organization also offers support groups for trans and nonbinary youth and adults. It provides guidance and resources to families who are navigating a family member's transition or gender identity.

GLSEN is a nonprofit organization that advocates for LGBT inclusion and rights in the United States K–12 education system, working to help LGBT students, educators, and school administrators feel safe and accepted at school. The organization also speaks out against discriminatory laws such as laws in seven US states that forbid educators from "promoting" same-sex relationships by talking about them in a positive way.[64] GLSEN also encourages the development of curricula and resources that help students learn about LGBT people and LGBT issues in a positive, supportive way. For example, the organization offers an hour-long lesson plan on a timeline of LGBT history and guides for educators on discussing gender in an LGBT-inclusive way.

One frontier for LGBT education and advocacy is LGBT-inclusive sex education. A report by the Public Religion Research Institute found that "among millennials surveyed in 2015, only 12 percent said their sex education classes covered same-sex relationships."[65] Along with organizations like GLSEN, the Human Rights Campaign has called for schools to close this gap and provide safe and comprehensive LGBT sex education for all students. But so far, few schools and organizations have taken the lead in providing these educational materials and resources for students.

Because of the historic cultural silence surrounding LGBT issues, it can be difficult for people to know how to support an LGBT friend or loved one. In 1972, Jeanne Manford decided to march publicly in support of gay rights alongside her son Morty. She met many LGBT people whose own parents had disowned or abandoned them. In response, Manford and her son founded the organization PFLAG in 1973. PFLAG, which originally stood for "Parents, Family, and Friends of Lesbians and Gays," is an organization for families and allies of

LGBT people. PFLAG has more than 400 local chapters across the country where allies and families of LGBT people can meet. The organization also advocates for LGBT issues.

There are also online communities and resources for LGBT people and their allies. The website *Everyone Is Gay* is operated by Kristin Russo and Dan Owens-Reid, who began giving advice on a YouTube channel in 2010. Russo and Owens-Reid both identify as queer, and they draw on their own experiences as well as those of friends and loved ones while giving advice on their website. Other resources such as the online magazine *Scarleteen* and the website for the health organization Planned Parenthood, as well as LGBT-themed advice columns like *¡Hola Papi!* and *Ask a Queer Chick*, also offer guidance to LGBT people at all stages of life. Most of these resources agree that the most important way to support the LGBT community is with love and acceptance. *Everyone Is Gay* once answered a letter from a person looking to take the first step of coming out—coming out to themselves. Owens-Reid answered the letter in this way: "You don't come out to yourself. You slowly but surely figure out the things you want in life. You feel more and more comfortable going against everything people are trying to force you to feel."[66]

❝You feel more and more comfortable going against everything people are trying to force you to feel.❞ [66]

—*Dan Owens-Reid, advice columnist on* Everyone Is Gay, *on the process of accepting sexuality*

SOURCE NOTES

INTRODUCTION: NOT SAFE TO LEARN

1. Liv Funk, "A Police Officer at My Public High School Told Me I'm Going to Hell Because I'm Gay," *ACLU*, May 21, 2018. www.aclu.org.

2. Funk, "A Police Officer at My Public High School Told Me I'm Going to Hell."

3. Funk, "A Police Officer at My Public High School Told Me I'm Going to Hell."

4. Quoted in Mary Emily O'Hara, "Two Queer High School Girls Got Their Principal Fired After Years of Discrimination," *Them*, May 23, 2018. www.them.us.

5. Funk, "A Police Officer at My Public High School Told Me I'm Going to Hell."

CHAPTER 1: WHAT IS THE HISTORY BEHIND LGBT INTOLERANCE?

6. Quoted in Janet Maslin, "Looking at a Novelist's Career While Keeping a Close Eye on His Sexuality," *New York Times*, May 17, 2010. www.nytimes.com.

7. Quoted in R. B. Parkinson, *A Little Gay History: Desire and Diversity Across the World*. New York: Columbia UP, 2013. p. 15.

8. "Genesis 13:13," *Bible Study Tools*, n.d. www.biblestudytools.com.

9. Quoted in Catherine Butler, Amanda O'Donovan, and Elizabeth Shaw, *Sex, Sexuality and Therapeutic Practice: A Manual for Therapists and Trainers*. New York: Routledge, 2010. p. 103.

10. *Stonewall Uprising*. Directed by Kate Davis and David Heilbroner, Q Ball Productions for American Experience, 2010.

11. Quoted in Tyler Austin, "Today in Gay History: Gay Activist Pies Anita Bryant in the Face," *Out*, October 14, 2016. www.out.com.

12. "Silence=Death," *ACT UP*, n.d. www.actupny.org.

13. Quoted in Jen Christensen, "AIDS in the '80s: The Rise of a New Civil Rights Movement," *CNN*, June 1, 2016. www.cnn.com.

14. "Obergefell v. Hodges," *Supreme Court of the United States*, June 26, 2015. www.supremecourt.gov.

CHAPTER 2: HOW IS SOCIETY INTOLERANT OF LGBT PEOPLE?

15. Mark Shrayber, "I Came Out to My Homophobic Parents," *Bold Italic*, August 24, 2014. www.thebolditalic.com.

16. Shrayber, "I Came Out to My Homophobic Parents."

17. Sarah Schulman, *Ties that Bind: Familial Homophobia and Its Consequences*. New York: The New Press, 2009. p. 62.

18. Schulman, *Ties that Bind*, p. 19.

19. Quoted in Christine Hauser, "Texas Teacher Showed a Photo of Her Wife and Was Barred from the Classroom," *New York Times*, May 10, 2018. www.nytimes.com.

20. Quoted in Diane Smith and Bill Hanna, "Embattled Gay Teacher Is Back in a Mansfield Classroom, but Her Fight's Not Over Yet," *Fort Worth Star-Telegram*, August 9, 2018. www.star-telegram.com.

21. Quoted in Ria Tabacco Mar and Emma J. Roth, "Chili's Denied Meagan Hunter a Promotion Because She Needed to 'Dress More Gender Appropriate,'" *ACLU*, January 16, 2019. www.aclu.org.

22. Quoted in Mar and Roth, "Chili's Denied Meagan Hunter a Promotion."

23. Quoted in Jenny Roper, "John Browne on Being Out at Work," *HR*, September 25, 2015. www.hrmagazine.co.uk.

24. Quoted in Jacey Fortin, "A 12-Year-Old Came Out to Her Mormon Church. Then Her Mike Was Cut Off," *New York Times*, June 22, 2017. www.nytimes.com.

25. Quoted in Fortin, "A 12-Year-Old Came Out to Her Mormon Church."

26. Quoted in Julie Compton, "Fighting Irish: Battle for LGBTQ Inclusion in St. Patrick's Day Parades Continues," *NBC News*, March 13, 2018. www.nbcnews.com.

27. Quoted in Hilary Weaver, "Ellen DeGeneres's Groundbreaking Coming Out: 20 Years Later," *Vanity Fair*, April 28, 2017. www.vanityfair.com.

28. Quoted in Bennett Singer and David Deschamps, *LGBTQ Stats: Lesbian, Gay, Bisexual, Transgender, and Queer People by the Numbers*. New York: The New Press, 2017. p. 192.

29. Quoted in Hugh Ryan, "Why So Many Disney Villains Sound 'Gay,'" *Vice*, July 14, 2015. www.vice.com.

30. Quoted in Ryan, "Why So Many Disney Villains Sound 'Gay.'"

31. "Healthcare Equality Index 2018," *Human Rights Campaign*, 2018. www.hrc.org.

CHAPTER 3: HOW DOES INTOLERANCE HURT LGBT PEOPLE?

32. Quoted in Ryan Roschke, "Why Ashlee Marie Preston's 34th Birthday as a Transgender Woman Is a Huge Deal," *PopSugar*, June 19, 2018. www.popsugar.com.

33. Quoted in Roschke, "Why Ashlee Marie Preston's 34th Birthday as a Transgender Woman Is a Huge Deal."

34. Quoted in Michael Tarm, Associated Press, "Transgender Inmate Gets Rare Transfer to Female Prison," *U.S. News & World Report*, December 27, 2018. www.usnews.com.

35. Quoted in James Michael Nichols, "6 Homeless LGBTQ Youths Share Their Stories," *Huffington Post*, June 14, 2018. www.huffingtonpost.com.

36. Quoted in Nichols, "6 Homeless LGBTQ Youths Share Their Stories."

37. "LGBTQ," *National Alliance on Mental Illness*, n.d. www.nami.org.

38. Quoted in Anthony DeCurtis, "Rufus Wainwright Journeys to 'Gay Hell' and Back," *New York Times*, August 31, 2003. www.nytimes.com.

39. Quoted in Laura Bullard, "Battling My Body: Being Queer with an Eating Disorder," *Marie Claire*, March 1, 2018. www.marieclaire.com.

40. Daniel Ortberg, "The Best $6,250 I Ever Spent: Top Surgery," *Vox*, December 18, 2018. www.vox.com.

41. Ortberg, "The Best $6,250 I Ever Spent."

42. Daniel Ortberg, *Twitter*, 12:17 p.m., January 9, 2019. www.twitter.com/danielortberg.

43. Quoted in IFC Films, "Do I Sound Gay? – Official Trailer | HD | Sundance Selects," *YouTube*, June 3, 2015. www.youtube.com.

44. Quoted in Ale Russian, "Amandla Stenberg Came Out as Gay After Battling 'Internalized Homophobia': 'I Was Scared,'" *People*, September 19, 2018. www.people.com.

45. Rachel Williams, "Why Internalized Transphobia Is the Hardest Battle," *Transphilosopher*, November 3, 2016. transphilosopher.wordpress.com.

CHAPTER 4: WHAT IS THE FUTURE OF GENDER AND SEXUAL EQUALITY?

46. Quoted in Patrick Crowley, "Ask the Artists: What Does Pride Mean in This Political Climate?" *Billboard*, June 11, 2017. www.billboard.com.

47. Sam Escobar, "How I Told the World I'm Neither a Man nor a Woman," *Esquire*, August 5, 2016. www.esquire.com.

48. Escobar, "How I Told the World I'm Neither a Man nor a Woman."

49. Masha Gessen, "Trump's Transgender Military Ban and Lessons from a Lifetime of Gender-Policing," *New Yorker*, January 23, 2019. www.newyorker.com.

50. Kimberly Mascott Zieselman, "I Was an Intersex Child Who Had Surgery. Don't Put Other Kids Through This." *USA Today*, August 9, 2017. www.usatoday.com.

51. Quoted in Katherine Hignett, "Who Is Sharice Davids? Kansas Democrat Become First Openly LGBT Native American Woman Elected to House," *Newsweek*, November 7, 2018. www.newsweek.com.

52. Quoted in J. P. Brammer, "Steven Universe Is the Queerest Animated Show on TV," *Vulture*, January 30, 2017. www.vulture.com.

53. Quoted in Curtis M. Wong, "The History and Meaning of the Rainbow Pride Flag," *Huffington Post*, June 7, 2018. www.huffingtonpost.com.

54. Quoted in Wong, "The History and Meaning of the Rainbow Pride Flag."

55. Quoted in "Coming Out by Cake: Girl Leaves Tasty Treat and Heartfelt Letter Telling Parents She's Gay," *Huffington Post*, December 6, 2017. www.huffingtonpost.com.

56. Quoted in "Why Do This?" *VideoOut*, n.d. www.videoout.org.

57. Elijah C. Nealy, *Transgender Children and Youth: Cultivating Pride and Joy with Families in Transition*. New York: W. W. Norton & Company, 2017. p. 62.

58. Adam Rippon and Romy Oltuski, "Adam Rippon Explains Why Coming Out Is a Process That Never Ends," *InStyle*, June 29, 2018. www.instyle.com.

59. Quoted in "US Supreme Court Allows Trump Military Transgender Ban," *BBC News*, January 22, 2019. www.bbc.com.

60. Quoted in Adam Liptak, "Supreme Court Revives Transgender Ban for Military Service," *New York Times*, January 22, 2019. www.nytimes.com.

61. Quoted in Liptak, "Supreme Court Revives Transgender Ban for Military Service."

62. Quoted in "The State of LGBT Human Rights Worldwide," *Amnesty International*, n.d. www.amnestyusa.org.

63. Quoted in "Gay Chechens Flee Threats, Beatings, and Exorcism," *BBC News*, April 6, 2018. www.bbc.com.

64. Quoted in "'No Promo Homo' Laws," *GLSEN*, n.d. www.glsen.org.

65. Quoted in "A Call to Action: LGBTQ Youth Need Inclusive Sex Education," *Human Rights Campaign*, n.d. www.hrc.org.

66. Dan Owens-Reid and Kristin Russo, "How Do You Come Out . . . To Yourself?" *Everyone Is Gay*, August 12, 2015. www.everyoneisgay.com.

FOR FURTHER RESEARCH

BOOKS

Lillian Faderman, *The Gay Revolution: The Story of the Struggle*. New York: Simon & Schuster, 2015.

Heidi C. Feldman, *LGBT Discrimination*. San Diego, CA: ReferencePoint Press, 2019.

Elijah C. Nealy, *Transgender Children and Youth: Cultivating Pride and Joy with Families in Transition*. New York: W. W. Norton & Company, 2017.

Pat Rarus, *The LGBT Rights Movement*. San Diego, CA: ReferencePoint Press, 2019.

INTERNET SOURCES

"LGBT Youth," *American Civil Liberties Union*, n.d. www.aclu.org.

Annie Tritt, "States Are Starting to Recognize a Third Gender. Here's What That Means for Nonbinary Youth," *Vox*, April 2, 2018. www.vox.com.

Hilary Weaver, "Ellen DeGeneres's Groundbreaking Coming Out: 20 Years Later," *Vanity Fair*, April 28, 2017. www.vanityfair.com.

Curtis M. Wong, "The History and Meaning of the Rainbow Pride Flag," *Huffington Post*, June 6, 2018. www.huffingtonpost.com.

WEBSITES

Everyone Is Gay

www.everyoneisgay.com

Everyone Is Gay is an advice and resource center for LGBT people and their loved ones.

GLAAD

www.glaad.org

GLAAD is an organization that focuses on advocating for the representation of LGBT people in the media. Its goal is to "rewrite the script" of the portrayal of LGBT people in public life.

Human Rights Campaign

www.hrc.org

The Human Rights Campaign is an advocacy group for LGBT rights across the United States. It keeps track of developing human rights issues and conducts research on LGBT rights.

The Trevor Project

www.thetrevorproject.org

The Trevor Project offers suicide prevention and crisis services to young LGBT people. Its crisis hotline, 1-866-488-7386, is accessible 24/7.

INDEX

INDEX CONTINUED

IMAGE CREDITS

ABOUT THE AUTHOR

A.W. Buckey is a writer living in Brooklyn, New York.